Smelly Jokes

for kids

First published in Great Britain 1988 by Ward Lock Limited,

This edition published 2004 by Bounty Books,
a division of Octopus Publishing Group Ltd,
2-4 Heron Quays, London E14 4JP
Reprinted 2004

ISBN 0 7537 0880 9

Printed and Bound in China

Smelly Jokes
for kids

What do you call a man with cow droppings all over his shoes?

An incowpoop.

What did the grape do when the elephant sat on him?

He let out a little wine.

Knock, knock.
Who's there?
Halibut.
Halibut who?
Halibut coming out with me tonight?

Why does the big dinosaur have so few friends?

Because he Tyrannosaurus reeks.

Why did the idiot fail his driving test?

He opened the car door to let out the clutch.

Why do grape-harvesters have noses?

So they have something to pick during the growing season.

What's black and white, smells and bounces?

A skunk on a pogo stick.

Two old men were talking about how things had changed since they were young. 'I didn't kiss my wife before we were married, did you?' said one to the other.

'I can't remember,' said the second. 'What did you say her name was?'

A man walked into his house holding a cowpat in his hand.

'Look, everyone,' he cried. 'See what I almost stood on!'

Knock, knock.
Who's there?
Weevil.
Weevil who?
Weevil overcome. Weevil overcome some day...ay...ay...ay...ay.

What did the woodworm say when he walked into a pub?
'Is the bar tender here?'

Did you hear about the parachute?
It opens on impact.

What do ants put under their arms?
Anti-perspirant.

How did the flea get down from the skunk?
It didn't. You get down from a duck.

Alec: 'A bat bit me on the neck last night.'
Sam: 'Did you put anything on it?'
Alec: 'No, it seemed to like me unsalted.'

Alec: 'How do you keep a smelly schoolboy in suspense?'
Sam: 'I don't know.'
Alec: 'I'll tell you tomorrow.'

'Doctor, doctor, I smell like a bee.'
'Buzz off; I'm busy.'

Knock, knock.
Who's there?
Tina.
Tina who?
Tina sardines.

What's black and white, smells and is found at the North Pole?

A very lost skunk.

'What's the secret of living to be 100?' the reporter asked the elderly man.

'Slugs!' replied the elderly man.

'Slugs?' said the reporter.

'Yes! I've never eaten one in my life!'

Alec: 'My dad thinks he's a skunk.'
Sam: 'Has he seen a psychiatrist?'
Alec: 'Why should he? The smell keeps the burglars away.'

An angry customer in a restaurant complained that his fish was bad, so the waiter picked it up, smacked it and said, 'Naughty, naughty, naughty!'

Knock, knock.
Who's there?
Tuna.
Tuna who?
Tuna piano and it won't sound so bad.

Sam: 'Why did you buy a black and white dog?'
Alec: 'I couldn't afford a colour licence.'

What do you get if you cross a whale with rotten fish?
Moby Sick.

What do you call a baby that plops through the letter box?
Bill.

'Doctor, doctor, my wife says I smell like a goat!'
'Really! And how do the kids smell?'

Did you hear about the flea that failed its exams?
It couldn't come up to scratch.

Knock, knock.
Who's there?
Kipper.
Kipper who?
Kipper smelly jokes to yourself.

What did the lobster say to the rock-pool?
'Let me see your muscles.'

What's tall and smells nice?
A giraffe-odil.

'Those currant buns you sold me yesterday had three cockroaches in them,' a woman complained over the phone to a baker.

'Sorry about that,' said the baker. 'If you bring the cockroaches back, I'll give you the three raisins I owe you.'

What do you get if you cross a mole with a skunk?
Smelly tunnels.

'Waiter, waiter, how do you serve shrimps here?'
'We bend down, Sir.'

Alec: 'Are slugs tasty, Miss?'
Teacher: 'Get on with your lunch and keep quiet.'
Teacher (a little later): 'Now, what was that about slugs, Alec?'
Alec: 'It doesn't matter now, Miss. There was one in your salad, but you've eaten it.'

What do you call two sun-tanned men sitting in a shoebox?

A pair of brown loafers.

How many wallies does it take to peel an onion?

Two. One to hold the knife and one to turn the onion.

What do you get if you cross an owl with an oyster?

A creature that drops pearls of wisdom.

What do you call a man sitting on the doorstep?

Mat.

How do you stop a skunk from charging?
Take away its credit card!

Why was the banker sitting in a tree?
Because he had just been made branch manager.

Did you hear about the silly gardener who broke his arm raking leaves?
He fell out of the tree!

'Doctor, doctor, everything I eat comes up.'
'Quick! Eat my Premium Bonds!'

'Waiter, waiter, what's the meaning of this smelly soup?'
'I don't know, Sir. I read tea-leaves, not soup plates.'

Alec: 'My dog's sick. It goes 'Tick! Tick!' instead of barking.'
Vet: 'Well, you said it was a watchdog.'
Alec: 'But why is it running round in circles?'
Vet: 'Because it's very wound up.'

Did you hear about the messy horse?
He had dreadful stable manners.

Alec: 'My new pet cost £10,000. It's part cat and part bull.'
Sam: 'Which part's the bull?'
Alec: 'The bit about it costing £10,000.'

Why did the woman put her two sons on her husband's stomach?
She was trying to put heirs on his chest.

Alec: 'Did you hear about the famous lion tamer whose best trick was to stick his left arm in the lions' mouths? He was called Fearless Fred.'
Sid: 'What do they call him now?'
Alec: 'Mr Right!'

What's the most critical of all animals?
The moth, because it picks holes in everything.

Which gangster smelt of fish?
Al Caprawn.

What's brown and goes 'splat'?
A cowpat falling off a cliff.

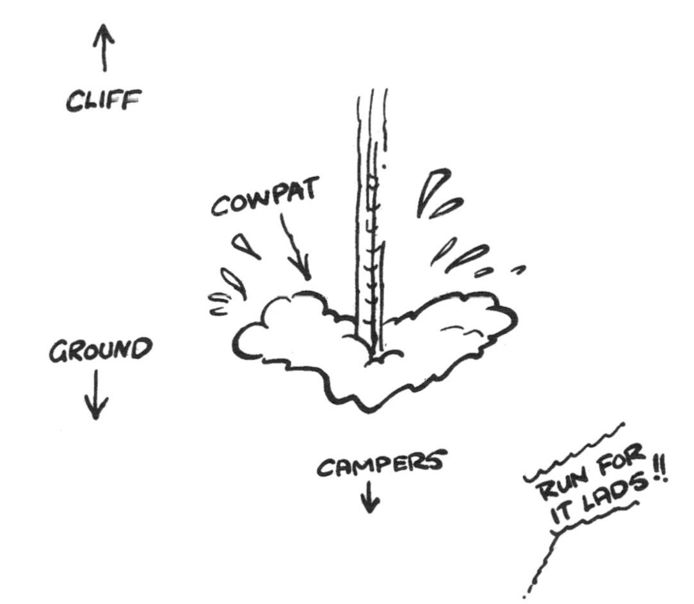

What do you call a man sitting in a pile of autumn leaves?

Russell.

How do you stop a pig from smelling?

Put a clothes-peg over its nose.

'Has your dog ever had fleas?'

'No, but it had a litter of puppies three weeks ago.'

Sam: 'Your dog smells dreadful! Call him off.'
Alec: 'We've called him 'Henry' since he was a puppy. It's a bit late to change now.'

What happened when a dog went to the flea circus?

It stole the show.

What's the best cure for a runny nose?

A tap on the head.

'Why is your son crying?' the doctor asked a young woman in his surgery.

'He has four baked beans stuck up his nose,' replied the woman.

'And why is his little sister screaming?' asked the doctor.

'She wants the rest of her lunch back,' said the woman.

A girl stood on the bridge one night.
Her lips were quite a-quiver.
She gave a cough, her head fell off
And floated down the river.

First cannibal: 'I don't know what to make of my wife today.'
Second cannibal: 'How about sandwiches?'

Did you hear about the man who swallowed a tin of varnish?
He had a lovely, glossy finish.

'Doctor, doctor, my wife said I smell like a motor car.'

'Well, you do look a bit exhausted.'

Why did the dog have her puppies in the dustbin?

Because it said: PLACE LITTER HERE.

'Doctor, doctor, I have terrible dandruff.'

'Best not to tell anyone about it.'

'What do you mean?'

'Keep it under your hat!'

Why are smelly schoolboys like face flannels?

Because they both shrink from washing.

What's the best thing for smelly feet?
A foot-pump!

First cannibal: 'Am I late for lunch?'
Second cannibal: 'Not at all. Nobody's eaten yet.'

'Doctor, doctor, my best friend told me I had B.O.!'
'And what makes you think he's right, you disgusting, smelly, foul little man?'

What has one wheel, two legs and smells?
A barrow full of manure.

Little Alec, bad as Hell,
Dropped his sister in the well.
Mother said, while drawing water,
'Gosh, it's hard to raise a daughter.'

'Doctor, doctor, what can you give me for my kidneys?'
'I've got some eggs and bacon in the fridge.'

'Doctor, doctor, what can I do about my bad breath?'
'Stop breathing!'

Why do people who snore smell of fish?
Because they're kippers.

The bottle of perfume that Willie sent,
Was highly displeasing to Millicent.
Her words were quite cold,
And they argued I'm told,
'Bout the silly scent Willie sent Millicent.

Did you hear about the snake with the bad cold?
It had to viper nose.

'Doctor, doctor, I've a button up both my nostrils. What can I do?'
'Try breathing through the little holes.'

What has twelve legs, two eyes and smells of fish?
Three blind mice and a kipper.

'Doctor, doctor, I tend to flush an awful lot.'
'Don't worry. It's a normal chain-reaction.'

What happened when the cat ate the cheese?
It waited for the mouse with baited breath.

'You've got the worst B.O. I've ever smelt,' said the doctor. 'You need a major operation.'

'I'd like a second opinion, please.'

So the doctor sniffed and said, 'You've got the worst B.O. I've ever smelt. You need a major operation!'

Knock, knock.
Who's there?
Ammonia.
Ammonia who?
Ammonia bird in a gilded cage.

'Doctor, doctor, I smell like a lump of Cheddar!'
'Hard cheese!'

Who says, 'I'm out! Plop!'?
A poker player throwing his hand in.

'Doctor, doctor, why do I smell like a custard?'
'You don't. You're just being thick.'

Official: 'What's your name?'
Man at desk: 'Fred Pongs.'
Official: 'What do you want to change it to?'
Man at desk: 'Michael.'
Official: 'Fred Michael?'
Man at desk: 'No! Michael Pongs.'

'I'm very worried about my little boy's nail biting habit,' a woman said to her doctor.

'Nail biting is very common in youngsters,' said the doctor.

'What? Six-inch rusty ones?' said the woman.

'Docor, doctor, I smell like a dog.'

'Sit down for a minute.'

'But I'm not allowed on the furniture.'

The Queen of Hearts, she made some tarts
In a pretty, pink porcelain basin.
Alay! Alack! She turned her back,
And her spaniel dipped its face in.

'Dentist, dentist, that mouthwash you gave me for my bad breath makes my gums smart.'

'Perhaps you'd better try rubbing some on your head then!'

'Doctor, doctor, I smell like a cup of coffee.'
'What's got into you?'
'A little cream and one sugar.'

Which insects smell nice?
Deodor-ants.

What's black and white, pongs and hangs from a line?

A drip-dry skunk.

Did you hear about the new prize for people who cure themselves of B.O.?

It's called the No-smell prize.

'Doctor, doctor, how can I stop my daughter biting her nails?'

'Buy her some shoes.'

'Doctor, doctor, every time I drink a cup of tea I get a sharp pain in my nose.'

'Have you tried taking the spoon out of the cup?'

Which Star Wars character had B.O.?

Darth Odour.

What smells of fish and chases criminals?

A squid car.

'Doctor, doctor, my husband's off his food.'

'Gosh! How long was he sitting on it for?'

'Doctor, doctor, my family think I'm mad because I prefer brown shoes to black shoes.'

'What's wrong with that? So do I!'

'Boiled or fried?'

What did the white blood cell say to the red blood cell?

'Wanna come to my plasma?'

The food at the club dinner was awful. The soup tasted like dishwater, the fish was off, the meat was overcooked and the vegetables were obviously old. The last straw for one member was the thick, lumpy custard. 'This meal is disgusting!' he roared. 'And what's more, I'm going to bring it up at the club meeting tomorrow!'

Did you hear about the lorry load of smelly glue that spilled on to the M1?

The police asked motorists to stick to their own lanes.

What do you call a baby prawn that won't let others play with its toys?

Shellfish.

What do pigs do if they get sore eyes?

They rub oinkment in them.

Did you hear about the boy who wrote 'knickers' on his fingers?

He was caught rude handed.

'Doctor, doctor, what are the chances of this diet working?'

'Very slim.'

What team does Hissing Sid support?

Slitherpool.

What do royal nudists get on their birthdays?

21 bum salutes.

PROTEST!

ONLY 14 BUMS
SHOWN HERE, AS SMART
ALEXANDER THINKS THIS
JOKE TO BE CHEEKY!

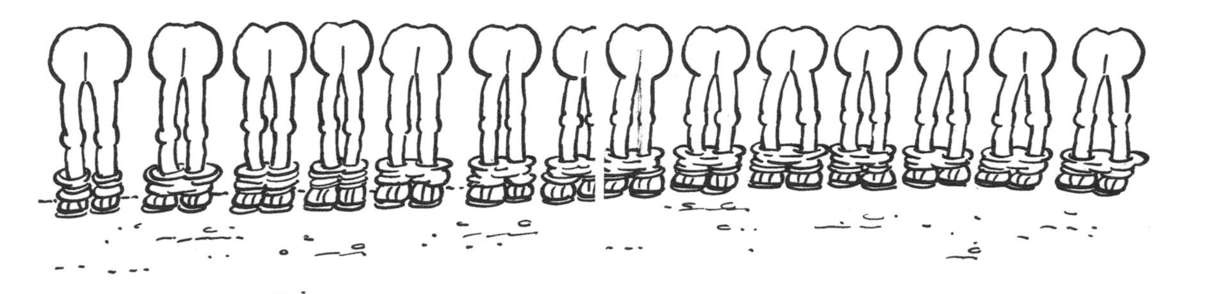

Which ancient warrior smelt like a pig?
Attila the Ham.

What smells of fish and helps you hear?
A herring-aid.

Why do vampires use a mouthwash?
So they won't get bat teeth.

Which famous painter always had a bad cold?
Vincent van Cough.

What's grey, has four legs, tusks, a trunk and sprays its enemies?
A skunk disguised as an elephant.

What's black and white, smells and goes up and down?
A skunk holding a yo-yo.

What's a monster's favourite drink?
Gin and slime.

Did you hear about the man with grease stains all over his shirt?
He had a chip on his shoulder.

What's black and white, pongs and has four wheels?
A skunk on a skateboard.

What did the mosquito say when he saw the man having a lie-in?
'Ah! Breakfast in bed!'

What do you call a monster sitting in the gutter?
Dwayne.

What do you call a monster with a boulder in each ear?

Anything you like. It can't hear you!

What's smelly and takes aspirins?

A skunk with a headache.

A man walked into a chemist shop and said, 'I'd like something to take this smell away.'

'Oh, so would I, Sir,' said the chemist, wafting his hands. 'So would I.'

Teacher: 'What's the difference between select and choose, Alec?'

Alec: 'Select is when we pick something. Choose is what's on our feet.'

What smells sweet and swings from the trees?
A meringue-utan.

Did you hear about the skunk that couldn't spray?
It ran out of gas.

What do you get if you cross a skunk with a can of Right Guard?
A monster's deodorant.

What do you get if you cross a kangaroo with a skunk?

A jumper that needs a good wash.

What's the difference between a skunk and a biscuit?

Ever tried dunking a skunk in your tea?

Smelly man: 'What would I have to give you to get a kiss?'
Girl: 'An anaesthetic.'

What do you get if you cross a vampire with a skunk?

A sucker with B.O.!

'Doctor, doctor, how long can someone live with bad breath?'

'I don't know! How old are you?'

What would you get if you cross a watchdog with a skunk?

Smelly postmen.

Why is a pedestrian like a piece of lavatory paper?

When all is passed safely, you tear across the dotted line.

What happened when the workers at the false-nose factory went on strike?

Everyone went to picket.

What did the lion say when the skunk sprayed it?
Nothing. Lions can't talk.

Doctor: 'I can't diagnose the cause of your bad breath. It must be the alcohol.'
Patient: 'O.K. I'll come back when you're sober.'

Did you hear about the man who was found climbing on the roof of a pub?
He was told that the drinks were on the house.

Did you hear about the gravediggers who went on a go-slow?

They decided they'd only deal with emergency cases.

'My brother's got a Rolls Royce nose.'

'What do you mean?'

'You can't hear it run.'

What smells most in a chemist shop?

Your nose.

Two caterpillars were crawling along a twig when a butterfly flew by.

'You know,' said one caterpillar to the other, 'when I grow up, you'll never get me in one of those.'

A man with a newt on his shoulder walked into a pub.

'What do you call him?' asked the barman.

'Tiny,' said the man.

'Why do you call him Tiny?' asked the barman.

'Because he's my newt!' replied the man.

'My grandfather has bunk-bed teeth.'

'What do you mean, 'bunk-bed teeth'?'

'One on top and one below.'

What's a cow's favourite game?
Moosical chairs.

Did you hear about the policeman with B.O.?
He was the pong arm of the law.

Great Aunt Sally's parrot hadn't said a word since she bought it thirty years ago. One day, she was startled to hear the parrot squawk, 'This piece of lettuce is bad!'

'You *can* talk!' gasped Great Aunt Sally. 'Why haven't you said anything for thirty years?'

'Well,' said the parrot, 'the food's always been fresh until now.'

A lady bought twenty mothballs from a chemist shop. Next day, she bought another twenty.

'You must have lots of moths,' said the assistant.

'Not really. It's just that my aim isn't very good,' said the lady.

'The walls in my flat are very thin,' a woman complained to her friend.

'You mean you can hear everything going on next door?'

'Not just that: when they peel onions, I start to cry!'

Speaker: 'Order! Order!'
New M.P: 'Fish and chips twice, please!'

'Waiter, waiter, I don't like the flies in here.'

'Then come back tomorrow, we'll have some new ones by then.'

Which soldiers smell of salt and pepper?

Seasoned troopers.

'It says in this book that Eskimos eat raw fish and blubber.'

'I'm not surprised. You'd blubber too if you had to eat raw fish!'

Smelly Denny: 'Sob! My wife left me when I was in the bath last night.'
Benny: 'She must have been waiting years for the chance.'

What do you get if you cross a chicken with a skunk?

Fowl breath.

Which singer smells of fish?

A bass.

Why do handkerchief makers like inquisitive people?

Because they're always sticking their noses into their business.

'Look,' said the doctor to the patient on the phone, 'I'm sorry to hear that you've come out in boils, and it's very sad that you've fallen and broken your leg. But you know I don't make housecalls, Mother.'

What's green, has four legs and two trunks?
Two seasick tourists.

What did the cod say to the smelly haddock at the fish shop?
'Hello! Long time no sea!'

'Why do you call your puppy 'Nose'?'
'Because it runs all over the place.'

Shop assistant: 'Can I help you?'
Customer: 'Yes, I'd like a bath for a baby with a stainless-steel bottom, please.'
Shop assistant: 'Certainly. And what would you like the bath to be made of?'

Why did the Arran jumper smell so bad?
Because it was a heavy sweater.

Who holds smelly fish to ransom?
A kippernapper.

'Why did you lick your little sister?'
'Because you said little girls are made of sugar and spice and all things nice,' said the little boy. 'Well she isn't. She tastes awful!'

What did the mouse say to the smelly cheese?
'Well, I won't say it's been nice gnawing you!'

How do fish learn to count?
On their fish fingers.

'What are you doing in the chemist's shop?'
'I'd like something for my bad breath.'
'I don't think he'll give you very much for it.'

Why was the monk covered in grease?
Because he was the head friar.

What do you get if you cross the sun and a toad?
Star warts.

Lawyer: 'You may as well plead guilty to the charge of breaking into the fish-shop. Your suit stinks of fish!'
Accused: 'But that's not fair. I wasn't wearing this suit when I did it!'

What's the best way to stop cream going off?
Don't milk the cow.

'I saved hundreds of lives during the war,' boasted Alec's grandad.
'Gosh, how did you do that?' asked Alec.
'I put the cook in prison!'

Did you hear about the glassblower who sucked when he should have blown?
He got panes in his stomach.

‘I’m sorry, but I left a sponge in you when I operated last week,’ said the surgeon.

‘Oh, I wondered why I was so thirsty all the time!’ replied the patient.

‘Five pounds for one question!’ said the woman to the fortune teller. ‘That’s very expensive, isn’t it?’

‘Next!’

What do you call it if your parachute fails to open?

Jumping to a conclusion!

'Run!' shouted the missionary. 'Cannibals!'

'Don't panic,' said his companion. 'Let's not get ourselves in a stew!'

'I was born in 1985,' said the elderly lady.

'Oh, come now,' said the vicar.

'I was,' said the lady. 'And my sister was born right next door in room 1986.'

Sunday school teacher: 'Never do anything in private that you wouldn't do in public.'
Alec: 'Great! No more baths.'

Teacher: 'What are the four seasons, Alec?'
Alec: 'Salt, pepper, mustard and vinegar, Miss.'

'Has anyone got an unusual pet?' asked the teacher one day.

'I've got a dog with no nose,' said one boy.

'Gosh! How does it smell?'

'Horrible!'

Mum: 'Why are you making faces at the bulldog, Alex?'
Alec: 'Well, he started it!'

Why is perfume obedient?

Because it is scent wherever it goes.

'Did you hear about the health fanatic who lived on garlic alone?'

'I'm not surprised. Anyone who lives on garlic would have to live alone!'

Waiter: 'I've got a nice smelly Brie.'
Customer: 'I don't care if you've got measles. Just bring me the menu!'

Waiter: 'I've taken great pains over this salad.'
Diner: 'I know. I've got them now.'

How many drops of ammonia can you put in an empty test-tube?
One. Because after that it's not empty.

'Do long noses run in your family?' asked Alec's friend.
'Only when we've all got colds,' said Alec.

If your nose runs and your feet smell, what's wrong with you?
You were built upside-down.

A husband came home from work and said to his wife, 'Is that perfume I smell?'
'It is,' she said. 'And you do!'

'How's your nose?'

'Oh, shut up!'

'So's mine. Do you think we're both going down with a cold?'

'What's your new perfume called?' asked a man.

'High Heaven,' replied his girlfriend.

'I asked what it's called, not what it smells to!'

What's the smelliest game in the world?

Ping-Pong.

‘Do you see that snobbish Mrs Featherstone-Mainwaring?’ asked Alec’s mother. ‘Why does she always walk around with her nose in the air?’

‘I know,’ said Alec. ‘So she can’t smell that horrible perfume she wears.’

How do skunks behave in a crisis?

In*stink*tively.

‘You, boy!’ called a policeman. ‘We’re looking for a man with a huge red nose called Cotters!’

‘Really!’ said the boy. ‘What’re his ears called?’

Why do lions eat raw meat?

Because they don’t know how to cook!

The boy at the next desk to Alec had a cold and his sniffing was getting on Alec's nerves. 'Please, Miss,' he said to his teacher. 'Could you tell Billy to wipe his nose, 'cos his brain is leaking!'

What's the smelliest dog in the world?

A pongeranian.

What's worse than breaking an egg for breakfast and finding it's off?

Breaking two eggs for breakfast and finding they're both off.

'Did you hear about the man with B.O. who took two aspirins?'

'That wouldn't stop his B.O., would it?'

'Of course not. But he had a stinking cold.'

'I had my gas bill this morning.'

'Was it high?'

'High! It was so high, I exploded!'

What's green, slimy and goes hith?

A snake with a lisp.

Did you hear about the man with amnesia who broke wind?

It all came back to him.

Alec: 'Why are skunks so argumentative?'
John: 'Tell me.'
Alec: 'Because they like raising a stink.'

What do you get if you cross a missile with a skunk?

Stink bombs.

Why is a smelly cat like a fire?

Because the quicker you put them out the better.

Did you hear about the man whose nose was eleven inches long?

He was petrified that if it grew another inch it would turn into a foot!

How many drops of acetic acid does it take to make a stink bomb?

Quite a phew.

Alec: 'Did you hear about the television show to find the best smell in Europe?'
Mum: 'Don't be silly.'
Alec: 'Honest, Mum. It's called 'The European Pong Contest.'

What did the skunk say to its mate when they were trapped?

Let us spray.

Did you hear about the girl who sat under the cow?

She got a pat on the head.

What fur do you get from a skunk?

As fur away as possible.

A young girl, all bright and breezy,
Said that eating raw onions was easy.
She ate twenty-two,
Rushed off to the loo,
'Cos she looked and felt terribly queasy.

'What do you call a smelly bear?
Winnie the Poooooooooooh!

'Doctor, doctor, these pills you gave me for bad breath aren't working.'
'Why not?'
'Because I can't get the lid off the bottle.'

Alec: 'Have you heard the joke about the dung-heap?'
Tony: 'No! Was it funny?'
Alec: 'It was a load of old rubbish.'

Why is a ripe cheese like a piece of steel?
Because they're both smelt.

Did you hear about the wally who thought Chanel Number 5 was one of the new television stations?

Alec: 'What do you call a smell that's afraid of the dark?'
Simon: 'No idea.'
Alec: 'A nervous reek.'

Knock, knock.
Who's there?
Odour.
Odour who?
Odour red, red robin comes bob, bob bobbin along.

'My girlfriend had a nasty accident in the kitchen last night!'

'What happened?'

'She forced me to eat it as usual!'

What did the Ancient Greeks shout when Archimedes fell in a dung-heap?

You reeka! You reeka!

'Did you hear about the gents lavatory attendant who married the ladies' lavatory attendant?'

'Yes, it was a marriage of convenience.'

What's purple and hums?

A rotten plum.

What's the smelliest drink in the world?
Slime-juice.

'Smells are quite invisible,' said the chemistry teacher. 'We can't see them and we can't touch them.'

"That's not what you said last week,' said a pupil.

'Don't be silly. What did I say last week?'

'You said if we didn't behave, you would kick up a stink!'

When do babies laugh most?
When it's nappy time.

Did you hear about the taxi-driver who found a pair of kippers in the back of his cab?
The police told him that if no one claimed them within six months, he could have them back.

Mum: 'Why did you put that skunk in your sister's bed?'
Alec: 'Because I couldn't find a ferret!'

What do you get if you cross Alec's shoes with a banana?

Smelly slippers.

Alec: 'I just swallowed a bluebottle.'
Susie: 'Shouldn't you take something for it?'
Alec: 'No! I'll just let it starve.'

Annie: 'Whenever I feel down in the dumps I get myself something to wear.'
Danny: 'Is that why you smell like a rubbish-tip?

Customer: 'Waiter! This meat if off. It isn't fit for a pig.'
Waiter: 'Hang on a second and I'll get you something that is!'

Alec: 'You remind me of the sea.'
Anne: 'Because I'm wild and romantic with deep blue eyes?'
Alec: 'No! Because you smell like a rotten fish!'

How did Frankenstein become so popular?
He was always making new friends.

Visitor: 'Is your cat fond of children?'
Alec: 'Yes, but he'd rather eats rats.'

What did the boy maggot say to the girl maggot?
'What's a nice girl like you doing in a joint like this?'

How can you tell if an elephant has been sleeping in your bed?

The sheets are wrinkled and the bed smells of peanuts.

What's yellow and sniffs?

A banana with a cold.

What's the difference between a musician and a dead rat?

One composes and the other decomposes.

Alec: 'My cat smells really awful.'
Vet: 'Is it a tom?'
Alec: 'No, it's in this basket.'

What did one eye say to the other?

Just between ourselves, there's something that smells around here.

What's hot, romantic and smells of fat?

Chips that pass in the night.

Why did the audience come out of the theatre holding their noses?

Because they'd been watching a kitchen-sink drama.

'Doctor, doctor, my family thinks I'm mad because I like smelly cheese.'

'Nonsense! I like smelly cheese, too.'

'Oh, great! You must come and see my collection. I've got thousands of them.'

Why do bees have sticky hair?

Because they use honey combs.

Where do wasps go when they are ill?

To the waspital.

Patient: 'I hope I'm ill, doctor.'
Doctor: 'Why?'
Patient: 'I'd hate to be well and smell like this!'

A man walked into a fish shop and asked the fishmonger to throw him three mackerel.

'Why do you want me to throw them to you?' asked the fishmonger.

'So I can tell my kids I caught them!'

'That fish you've caught is a bit off, isn't it?' said one pelican to his mate.

'I know, but it fits the bill exactly.'

What's a mermaid?

A deep-she fish.

There was a young man called Art,
Who thought he'd be terribly smart.
He ate ten cans of beans,
And busted his jeans,
With a loud and earth-shattering ****!

Alec: 'Mum, the man next door has got cabbage coming out of his nose.'
Mum: 'How awful for him.'
Alec: 'Yes! He planted brussels sprouts.'

'Doctor, doctor, these pills you gave me for B.O...'
'What's wrong with them?'
'They keep slipping from under my arms!'

Why did the pig run away from the pigsty?

Because he felt that the other pigs were taking him for grunted.

Did you hear about the ghoul's favourite hotel?

It had running rot and mould in every room.

'Doctor, doctor, what can I do about my B.O.? It's so bad, even I can't stand it.'

'Why not try a clothes-peg on your nose like the rest of us.'

What did Noah say when he saw his sons fishing over the side of the Ark?

'Easy on the maggots, boys. I've only got one or two.'

'Doctor, doctor, my husband thinks he's a bottle of perfume.'

'Why didn't you bring him with you?'

'What, at sixty pounds an ounce!'

An apple a day keeps the doctor away.
An onion a day keeps the whole world at bay.

Thought for the day: Do all chickens have fowl breath?

'Doctor, doctor, I keep thinking I'm a bad egg!'
'Well, the last time you came here, I told you to come out of your shell.'

Visitor: 'You're very quiet today, Alec.'
Alec: 'Yes, Mum promised to give me fifty pence if I didn't mention your B.O.!'

What's oriental, kills and smells?
Kung Phew.

'What's your new baby brother like?' a lady asked a boy whose mother had just given birth.
'I don't think he's finished yet,' said the boy.
'What makes you say that?'
'Because he leaks at both ends!'

Little birdie in the sky,
Dropping things from way up high.
Mr Farmer wiping eye,
Very thankful pigs can't fly!

Customer: 'Why is my food covered in smelly mud?'
Waiter: 'Well, you did ask me to step on it!'

Why did the bees in the swarm fly with their legs crossed?
They were looking for the nearest BP station!

What goes down during a bad attack of wind?
Half the trees in London and the south-east.

What would you call a boy who stepped on a cowpat?
Dungcan.

A dustman saw that someone had forgotten to put their bin out. He banged loudly on the door and eventually an upstairs window opened. 'Where's yer bin?' called the dustman as a sleepy-looking man peered out.

'Ah's bin out all night. Where's you bin?' yawned the man.

Where does a three-ton elephant with B.O. sleep?
Anywhere it wants to.

Teacher: 'What's the best way of preventing food from going bad?'
Pupil: 'Eating it while it's still fresh, Miss.'

Farmer: 'Have you anything for the maggots on my cow?'
Vet: 'If you tell me what's wrong with them, I'll have a look and see.'

Why do giraffes have such long necks?
Because their feet smell so bad.

How can you tell when cheese is off?
When it's past the smell-by date.

Customer: 'Waiter, this steak smells funny.'
Waiter: 'So why aren't you laughing?'

Teacher: 'Alec, how do you spell malodorous?'
Alec: 'M-a-l-l-o-d-r-u-s.'
Teacher: 'That's not how the dictionary spells it.'
Alec: 'You asked how I would spell it, Miss, not how the dictionary does!'

'Eureka!' shouted the scientist when he made an important discovery.

'Sorry, professor,' said his assistant. 'I didn't have time to shower this morning.'

'Did you hear about the scientist who invented a gas that's so strong it burns its way through anything?'

'No! What about him?'

'Now he's trying to invent something to keep it in!'

What do you call a multi-storey pig pen?

A styscraper.

What do skunks have that no other animals have?

Baby skunks.

'Which hand do you use to wipe your nose?'

'Actually, I always use a tissue. It's much more hygienic.'

'Did you hear about the two fleas that travelled from New York to San Francisco?'

'Don't tell me, they 'itch-hiked!'

Sarah: 'My flat-mate is threatening to move because everything I cook smells so awful.'
Jenny: 'Have you tried cooking books?'
Sarah: 'Do you grill them or fry them?'

'Waiter, this egg smells bad.'

'Don't blame me. I only laid the table.'

Why did the fish blush?
Because it saw the ship's bottom.

'Do skunks go on safari?
'Not safaris I know!'

Knock, knock.
Who's there?
Duncan.
Duncan who?
Duncan make your garden grow.

What's the difference between school dinners and pigs' swill?

Pigs' swill is served in buckets.

'Come on, Boris, eat your raw garlic. It's good for growing monsters.'

'But, Mum, I don't want to grow monsters!'

Why did the skunk soak its feet in a pink bucket?

Because it couldn't find its blue one!

The science teacher said to his class, 'If I add the white of a chicken's egg to that of a turkey's egg, I create a liquid that smells like a stink-bomb.' The class watched as the teacher mixed the two egg-whites together, but nothing happened! Which just goes to prove that two whites don't make a pong.

'Waiter, this milk smells off. Was it pasteurized?'
'No, Sir, just up to the top of the bottle!'

Alec: 'I bought a second-hand carpet yesterday. It was in mint condition.'
Sid: 'You mean it's as good as new?'
Alec: 'No, I mean it's got a hole in the middle.'

What comes out of the ground shouting 'Smelly feet! Smelly feet!'?

Crude oil.

'Doctor, doctor, my husband smells like a fish!'

'Poor sole!'

Alec: 'My dog's a dreadful bloodhound.'
Tim: 'Why's that?'
Alec: 'I cut my finger the other day and it fainted!'

Mum: 'Eat your cabbage, Alec. It'll put colour in your cheeks.'
Alec: 'Who wants green cheeks that smell of cabbage!'

What do you get if you cross a cod with a pair of gloves?
Fish fingers.

What do you get if you cross a pig with a flea?
Pork scratchings.

Alec: 'Have you heard the story of the body snatchers?'
Ann: 'No! Tell me!'
Alec: 'Better not. You might get carried away.'

What do you call a tiger that eats your mother's sister?
An aunt-eater.

Boy: 'Dad, there's a black cat in the kitchen!'
Dad: 'That's alright. Black cats are lucky.'
Boy: 'Not this one. It's just eaten Mum's fish pie.'

'What's the difference between a beautiful trout, cod and chips, and a pot of glue?'
'I don't know.'
'One's a dishy fish and the other's a fishy dish.'
'What about the pot of glue?'
'I knew you'd get stuck with that.'

What do you get if you cross an angler with a joker?

Fish and quips.

Why are there so many pigeons in railway stations?

Because they like to do a lot of train-spotting.

What smells of fish and goes 'Vroom! Vroom!'?'

A motor-pike.

‘I wish I liked your sister,’ said a cannibal to a friend at dinner one night.

‘Don’t worry about it,’ said the second cannibal. ‘Just eat the potatoes and gravy.’

‘What do you do?’ Dumb Dinah asked a young man at a party.

‘I’m a naval surgeon,’ replied the man.

‘Gosh! I had no idea that surgery was so specialized!’ cooed Dumb Dinah.

Knock, knock.
Who’s there?
Colin.
Colin who?
Colin the doctor to cure my bad breath.

Alec: 'Did you know that Mount Everest smells?'
Mum: 'Don't be silly.'
Alec: 'It does, honest! Teacher said it was the highest mountain in the world.'

A bird in the hand... means you've got to use the other hand to wipe your nose.

'Come here, boy!' roared the baker to the boy who had just thrown a stink-bomb into his shop. 'I'll teach you how to throw stink-bombs!'

'You don't have to,' said the boy. 'I can do it pretty well already.'

Teacher: 'You, boy! You must do something about your appearance!'
Boy: 'Why, Sir?'
Teacher: 'Because this is the first time you've put in an appearance this term!'

Where do you find giant snails?
On the end of a giant's fingers.

Alec: 'Did you hear the rumour about the rancid butter'
Dave: 'No, tell me!'
Alec: 'I'd better not, you might spread it.'

What cheese is made backwards?
Edam.

Why did the whale release Jonah?
Because it couldn't stomach him.

What's 2,000 square feet and smells of pigs?
The Common Market Swine Lake.

'Mrs Smith, I've cured Alec's runny nose.'
'How did you do that?'
'I stuck his fingers up his nostrils.'

A fish porter was walking through the market with three boxes of rotten fish on his head, whistling as he went.

'How on earth can you do that?' someone asked.

'Easy! I just purse my lips and blow!'

'Did you hear about the shipwrecked sailor who lived for two weeks on a tin of sardines?'

'Yes! On the fifteenth day he fell into the sea.'

'Doctor, doctor, I can't get to sleep at night. What shall I do?'

'Don't wash for a week.'

'Why not?'

'You'll soon hum yourself to sleep.'

Why does everything smell when it rains?
Because it's sweat outside.

What floats in space and smells of old kippers?
A nasteroid.

What's the best way to win at blow-football?
Eat garlic.

What do you get if you cross a Scottish legend and a bad egg?

The Loch Ness Pongster.

'What did Daddy say when he fell in the dung-heap?' a farmer's wife asked her son.

'Shall I leave out all the swear words?'

'Yes.'

'Nothing.'

A doctor told a woman that the only way to get rid of her bad B.O. was to bathe in milk every night for a week. But when she went back to the surgery a week later, the woman smelt even worse than before.

'Why didn't you do what I told you?' asked the doctor.

'I couldn't get in the bottle!' replied the woman.

What do you get if you cross a pig with a crusty pimple?

Warthogs.

Two cannibals were having lunch. 'Your wife makes a great soup,' said one to the other.

'Yes,' agreed the first. 'But I'm going to miss her terribly.'

‘Why are you feeding the baby with onions and beans for supper?’ a new granny asked her daughter.

‘So we can find him in the dark!’

‘My dog’s the laziest dog in the world!’

‘What makes you say that?’

‘Because when I’m watering the garden, he won’t lift a leg to help me.’

‘Did you hear about the cow that had hiccups?’

‘No!’

‘Hard cheese!’

How did Captain Hook die?

Picking his nose with the wrong hand.

'What do you get if you cross a crocodile with a flower?'

'I don't know, but I'm not going to smell it!'

What do you get if you cross a flea with a rabbit?

Bugs Bunny.

What do you get if you cross a nasty smell with a parasol?

A humbrella

'Dad!' cried Alec one morning. 'There's a woman at the door collecting for the children's home.'
'Tell her she can have you and your sister!'

'Do you say your prayers before meals?' the vicar asked a little boy.
'Not now my mum's cooking's improved!'

Sam: 'Why do you call your dog 'Miniature'?'
Alec: 'Because the miniature back's turned, he lifts his leg against the furniture.'

What do you call a man who sails to New York and back on the QE2 and never takes a bath?
A dirty double-crosser.

What do we get from naughty cows?
Bad milk.

What do you get if you cross a sneeze with a fish?
A cod in the nose.

'I've got some good news and some bad news!'
'Give me the bad news first, doctor.'
'I'm afraid we cut off the wrong leg!'
'What's the good news?'
'Your other leg is getting better.'

'There's an awful smell of B.O. in here,' said the new office-boy.

'It's the automatic air-conditioning,' said his boss. 'Whenever the weather gets hot it automatically breaks down!'

What happened when a van-load of dirty dishes went missing?

The police scoured the countryside.

Alec: 'What would you do if someone stole your perfume?'
Chemist: 'I'd put the police on the scent.'

What holds up stagecoaches and smells of fish?
Billy the Squid.

How do you cook sausages in the jungle?
Put them under a gorilla.

What do you call a pig that runs around with nothing on?

Streaky bacon.

'Have you heard about the man-eating lion?'

'No, but I heard about the man eating fish and chips.'

What happened when the Phantom of the Opera was sprayed by a skunk?

He wore a musk for ever after.

Why did the pig scratch itself?

Because no one else knew where it itched.

‘It’s raining cats and dogs outside,’ said Susie, looking out of the kitchen window.

‘I know,’ said her mum, who had just come in. ‘I’ve just stepped on a poodle!’

‘Shall I bring your dinner on deck?’ asked the steward.

‘No, just throw it overboard to save time.’

Why is a baby like a long piece of canvas?

They’re both wind-breakers.

What weighs over a ton, loves smelly mud and laughs a lot?

A happypotamus.

'Are you using your lawn-mower?' Mr Onthescrounge asked his neighbour one day.

'I was just about to,' said Jen O'Rosity, fed-up because he was always borrowing things.

'Oh, good!' said Mr Onthescrounge. 'You won't mind if I borrow your rake to mulch out the dung-heap then!'

Do you know how long cows should be milked?

For five minutes! The same as short ones!

What wouldn't you give a sick mouse with bad breath?

Mouse-to-mouse resuscitation!

What does a skunk call a fur coat that smells of mothballs?

Sweetheart.

Alec: 'I've just eaten an apple full of maggots!'
Sam: 'Do you want some water to wash them down?'
Alec: 'No, they can walk!'

'Do you love me, darling?' the groom asked his bride.

'I do, darling, I do!' said his new wife.

'And would you still love me if I had bad breath and B.O.?'

'I do, darling! I do!'

Why is being kissed by a vampire so unpleasant?

Because it has bat breath.

What did the female skunk say to the male skunk?

'Don't just stand there. Spray something!'

'Doctor, doctor, I'm worried. I keep thinking I smell of car fumes.'

'Come now, Sir. Don't exhaust yourself.'

Some of Alec's favourite books:
The Greedy Baby by Wendy Windbreaks
The Smelly Sneaker by O. Dereater
The Sweet Smell of Success by D. O. Derrant

'Any complaints?' asked the school dinner lady.

'My beans are as hard as rocks!' said one boy.

'They seem soft enough to me,' said the dinner lady, tasting a forkful.

'They would. I've been chewing them for ten minutes!' said the boy.

What's a polecat's favourite hobby?

Anything it can stink its teeth into.

What do you get if you cross an eagle with a skunk?

A bird that stinks to high heaven.

What did Billy Skunk say to Tommy Skunk's mum?
'Is Tommy coming out to spray today?'

There was a young man from South Ealing,
Who took a bus ride to Darjeeling.
It said on the door,
'Please don't spit on the floor'.
So he got up and spat on the ceiling!

Old Tom is gone! Alas! Alas!
He tried to trace escaping gas.
With lighted match he probed the meter,
Which blew him up to meet St. Peter.

What has a bottom at the top?
Your legs.

Knock, knock!
Who's there?
Felix.
Felix who?
Felix my nose once more, I'll scream!

Why was the smelly doctor so bad-tempered?
Because he was totally lacking in patients.

Why did the famous detective have yucky stuff on his chin?
Because Sherlock Foams.

Why did the tide turn?
Because the seaweed.

Why was Batman looking for worms?
Because Robin was hungry.

Mum: 'Your gran won't kiss you if you smell like that, Alec.'
Alec: 'I know. That's why I haven't taken a bath!'

Alec: 'Did you hear about the box of eggs?'
Sue: 'No!'
Alec: 'Too bad.'

When the cat's away... the house smells better!

'Doctor, doctor, I feel like a smelly old sock.'

'Well, I'll be darned!'

'Doctor, doctor! How can I cure my B.O.?'

'Take a cold bath every morning.'

'But I do, doctor.'

'Take a cold bath and fill it with nice, warm, soapy water.'

Did you hear about the millionaire with B.O.?

He was filthy rich.

Why did the thief take a bath?

Because he wanted to make a clean getaway.

'Waiter, there's a smelly film on my soup!'

'What do you want for fifty pence, 'The Sound of Music'?'

Why did the sailor grab a bar of soap when his ship sank?

So he could wash himself ashore.

A man walked into his doctor's office and said, 'You remember you told me to stay away from dampness until my rheumatism was better?'

'Yes,' said the doctor, holding his nose.

'Well, it's better. Can I have a bath now?'

Who was England's smelliest king?
William the Pongqueror.

Daddy Bear: 'Who's been sleeping in my bed?'
Baby Bear: 'Who's been sleeping in my bed?'
Mummy Bear: 'Shut up the pair of you! I just couldn't be bothered making them!'

What's green and fires rockets?
A septic tank.

What do lice do when they move scalps?
They throw a louse warming party.

Alec: 'Can I have a skunk for my brother?'
Pet-shop owner: 'Sorry, sonny. We don't do swaps here.'

Mum: 'Are you going to take a bath, Alec?'
Alec: 'No, Mum. I'll leave it where it is!'

There were two maggots sitting on Robinson Crusoe's knee.

'I'm off now,' said one.

'O.K.,' said the other. 'See you on Friday.'

What would you do if you found a skunk in your bed?

Tell it to sleep somewhere else.

Alec: 'I found a horseshoe today. Is it lucky?'
Mum: 'It might be for you, but what about the poor horse?'

'Did you hear about the smelly bed?'

'No, tell me about it.'

'I can't. It hasn't been made-up yet.'

Knock, knock.
Who's there?
Sonia.
Sonia who?
Sonia foot. I can smell it from here!

How do skunks get from place to place?
They fly by smellycopter.

Customer: 'A bar of soap, please.'
Chemist: 'Certainly, Sir. Scented or unscented?'
Customer: 'I think I'll just take it with me.'

'Waiter, I'd like some fish, please.'
'Hang on, Sir. I'll lay a plaice for you.'

An absent-minded professor brought a parcel into the lecture room. ‘I caught a frog and a toad yesterday and I’m going to discuss the difference between the two species,’ he said.

Opening the parcel, he brought out two mouldy cheese sandwiches.

‘Gosh!’ said the professor. ‘I could have sworn I ate my lunch yesterday.’

Mum: ‘Watch out for worms when you eat that apple, Billy.’
Billy: ‘They can jolly well watch out for themselves.’

Why is a fish shop always crowded?
Because the fish fillet.

'I'm going to change my psychiatrist tomorrow,' said a lady to her friend. 'He told me yesterday that I was in love with my perfume.'

'That does sound silly,' agreed the friend.

'Of course it is! I mean, we're very fond of each other. But *love*!'

'Waiter, what do you call this goo in my cup, coffee or tea?'

'What do you mean, Sir?'

'It smells like paraffin.'

'Oh, it's tea, then, Sir. Our coffee smells like paint-stripper!'

What town in Britain smells of rotting meat?

Oldham.

What's a sheep's favourite love song?
Will Ewe Still Love Me Tomorrow?

Why did the pig swill?
Because it saw the barn dance.

What's a pig's favourite love song?
I Only Have Styes For You.

Why does a cow flip its tail to get rid of flies?
Because that swat it's for.

What's sharp, smelly and dangerous?
Shark-infested vinegar.

Knock, knock.
Who's there?
Jupiter.
Jupiter who?
Jupiter have a bath tonight, you smell like an old kipper.

Who smells like a pig and puts people in pies?
Swiny Todd.

Who smells of fish and puts people in pies?
Sweeny Cod.

A man asked a chemist for something that smelled of rotten eggs, stale socks and sour milk.

'Why do you want something like that?' asked the chemist.

'I've got to leave my flat today and it states on the lease that I must leave it exactly as I found it!'

Who smells of frog spawn and puts people into pies?
Sweeny Toad.